DEFENDER

Brimming with creative inspiration, how-to projects and useful information to enrich your everyday life, Quarto Knows is a favourite destination for those pursuing their interests and passions. Visit our site and dig deeper with our books into your area of interest: Quarto Creates, Quarto Cooks, Quarto Homes, Quarto Lives, Quarto Drives, Quarto Explores, Quarto Gifts, or Quarto Kids.

First published in 2016 by Aurum Press
an imprint of the Quarto Group
The Old Brewery, 6 Blundell Street
London N7 9BH
United Kingdom

Text by Mike Gould

A catalogue record for this book is available from the British Library.

ISBN 978 1 78131 628 3
eISBN 978 1 78131 648 1

10 9 8 7 6 5 4 3
2020 2019 2018 2017

Edited by Philip de Ste. Croix
Designed by Paul Turner and Sue Pressley, Stonecastle Graphics Ltd
Cut-out images by PSDclip Ltd

Printed in China

DEFENDER

LAND ROVER'S LEGENDARY OFF-ROADER

MIKE GOULD

Contents

Introduction

The last Land Rover Defender rolled off the production lines at the company's Solihull plant on 29 January 2016, sixty-eight years after its direct antecedent, christened the 'Land-Rover', first left the same building. Over the course of its long production run, 2,016,933 of these iconic vehicles were built.

Its versatility was proven by the variety of roles it undertook and, as well as appealing to its intended utility customer base, its distinctive character found a ready market with leisure users too.

Its functional boxy shape rapidly made an impact all over the world, earning it the distinction that in many places the Land-Rover was the first vehicle people saw. The original basic model soon gave rise to many derivatives, including long- and extended-wheelbase models all built by combining elements of its modular design. Famously, the Defender – and Land Rover before it – saw frontline military service in conflicts around the world with British and foreign forces.

Overall, the vehicle comprehensively fulfilled its other key aim of earning export revenue. But perhaps its greatest accolade is that it gave its name to one of Britain's most successful companies.

◀ *A Land-Rover (right) and Series II on the Scottish Isle of Islay where the vehicle's name was coined.*

▶ *A Defender 110 Utility Station Wagon receives attention on the ramp at the Solihull factory.*

Chapter 1

Defender Heritage

Defender Dawning

Once the 'Land-Rover' project had been approved, development of a prototype using a Willys Jeep chassis and other parts proceeded rapidly. A Rover car engine replaced the Willys 'Go-Devil' unit with the main gearbox and axles also being car-derived. The rear axle was 'flipped' and modified to provide drive for the front wheels. A new permanent four-wheel-drive 2-speed transfer box was designed from scratch. It featured a flywheel device to provide a differential action which could be locked when driving off-road.

The solitary prototype was backed up by forty-eight pre-production vehicles built at Solihull that developed what would become an iconic design. Aluminium was used as it was freely available and easily formed, while the steel box-section chassis made expensive and complex tooling unnecessary.

All this was achieved in a matter of months over the winter of 1947–8 in the midst of severe postwar austerity.

▲ The BBC TV series Coast brought a Willys Jeep and the first pre-production Land-Rover HUE 166 together in Anglesey.

◄ Land-Rover pre-production number L09 was lovingly restored by Yorkshire-based vehicle expert Ken Wheelwright.

▶ The prototype was posed on the farm adjacent to the Solihull factory to emphasise its appeal to the farming market. The central steering position was quickly abandoned.

The Star of Solihull

The Land-Rover began production at Rover's factory at Solihull (near Birmingham) in March 1948 and ended with the last Defender rolling off the line in January 2016. Its home for those sixty-seven years remained the same. Block 1 of Solihull's South Works was built before the Second World War as a 'Shadow Factory' which could continue war material production in what was then open countryside should Britain's cities be bombed. Rover made the Bristol Hercules aircraft engine there during the war and moved car production to Solihull when hostilities ceased as its Coventry factory had been destroyed. The building still bears traces of wartime camouflage paint.

Employing freely available aluminium in the body and steel offcuts for the chassis, the pace of Land-Rover production was initially slow with only 1,758 vehicles coming off the line in the first year. By 1952

this number had risen to more than 20,000 but even at this level the company could not keep up with demand for the Land-Rover which had rapidly built up a healthy order book.

◄ *Early Land-Rovers on the assembly line in Solihull's South Works. To prove the concept, 48 pre-production vehicles were effectively hand built before committing to volume build.*

▲ *The pace rapidly built up with the company celebrating the 50,000th off the line in 1952.*

▶ *In January 2015, Land Rover opened a replica of the early Land-Rover production line as an attraction for visitors to the Solihull site. The 'Celebration Line' project brought in experts like Phil Bashall from Dunsfold Land Rover to ensure that the displays, including a virtually complete early vehicle, were authentic.*

VIP Vehicle of Choice

The Land-Rover rapidly gained a reputation for its capability and versatility. It was soon recognised as being ideal for a Royal review vehicle, leading to consternation at the BBC which, thanks to a prohibition on advertising, could only describe it as a 'field car'. Soon other celebrities became associated with the Land-Rover including prime minister Winston Churchill, and the film star Marilyn Monroe. Sophia Loren also used a Land-Rover on the set of the movie *El Cid*.

The brand's association with Royalty persisted throughout the model's life, even if others in the public eye later transferred their affections to its more luxurious sibling, the Range Rover.

▲ *Winston Churchill, then in his second term as prime minister, was presented with a Land-Rover on his eightieth birthday in 1954.*

▲ *The Royal Family quickly adopted the Land-Rover as a review vehicle, using this highly polished example to inspect the crew of aircraft carrier HMS* Albion *in 1957.*

▶ *Early Land-Rovers were exported to the United States with this one being used by Marilyn Monroe during a fashion shoot photographed by Sam Shaw on Long Island in 1957.*

Although often described as the 'first production Land-Rover', HUE 166 is actually the first Land-Rover ever. It was built at the start of a batch of pre-production vehicles in March 1948. It bears chassis number R01.

Rover's Success Story

The Rover Company soon realised that they had a winner on their hands with the Land-Rover. Its chairman, E. Ramson-Harrison, reported at the 1948 Annual General Meeting that the response to the new vehicle had been 'very satisfactory' and he offered the opinion that 'It may yet equal – and even exceed – our car output in quantity.' Its permanent four-wheel-drive system with a freewheel device soon gave way to a more conventional selectable transmission and the engines were upgraded to give more power. The petrol engines were joined by a specially designed diesel late in the model's life. The original Jeep-derived 80-inch wheelbase was increased to 86 inches in 1952. The range was further expanded by the introduction of a long 107-inch wheelbase variant in pick up and station wagon form, these changes leading to a peak in sales in 1955.

▲ *The Land-Rover was soon adopted for British military service to replace the wartime Jeep. This RAF Land-Rover dating from the 1950s has been superbly restored by enthusiast Nick Sawyer.*

◄ *The '107 Inch Station Wagon' looked extraordinary with its galvanised steel sections held together by a plethora of rivets. It could seat ten passengers and offered a de luxe trim option.*

Tickford Station Wagon

An early conversion of the Land-Rover was a station wagon derivative with a body built by coachbuilders Tickford Limited of Newport Pagnell. In an attempt to endow the Land-Rover with some of the luxury associated with Rover cars, Tickford created a leisure utility vehicle akin to the later Range Rover.

Rover supplied Tickford with a basic chassis and front end onto which the company fitted an aluminium body on a hardwood frame designed to resist tropical boring insects. Seven seats were squeezed into the 80-inch wheelbase, access to the rear being obtained by folding the passenger seat forward. The two-piece tailgate opened clamshell-style revealing small stowage areas for the wheel-changing equipment or a picnic snack, built into the wheelarch boxes. Other touches of luxury included floor covering with carpet on the transmission tunnel, a heater and dash stowage thanks to a one-piece windscreen.

▲ ▶ *The Tickford Station Wagon was stylish for its day with the bonnet-mounted spare wheel being concealed by a smart spun aluminium cover. Power came from the car-derived 1.6-litre petrol engine.*

As it was a station wagon rather than a utility vehicle, the Tickford Station Wagon attracted purchase tax in the home market so it wore a hefty £1,000 price ticket – then the price of a reasonably sized house. As a result sales in Britain were small but the vehicle was used extensively in overseas projects funded by the United Nations. Paid for in US dollars, this earned the country vital foreign currency.

Tickford produced more than 600 Station Wagons but the model was dropped in 1953 when Rover introduced its own considerably less stylish version.

◄ The rear tailgate was split to open top and bottom in the same way as the later Range Rover. The design featured body swaging hinting at the then popular 'Woody' style.

▲ The Rover Company's publicity department took the term 'Station Wagon' literally in their sales material. The location is said to be Olton Station near the Solihull factory.

Bold Adventurers

It did not take long for the Land-Rover to be recognised as the ideal vehicle for anyone planning a long-distance adventure. First to take to the road was the joint universities Oxford and Cambridge overland expedition to Singapore. Taking two Land-Rovers liveried in the appropriate shades of Varsity blue, a team of six completed the 29,000-kilometre journey in a little over six months.

They were followed by two remarkable individual adventurers. First on the trail was Group Captain Peter Townsend who went further, shipping his Land-Rover across oceans to cover the Americas and Africa. His book *Earth, My Friend* clearly reflected his troubled state of mind following his experiences as a pilot in the Battle of Britain and the trauma of a failed love affair with Princess Margaret.

◄ Members of the Oxford and Cambridge expedition to Singapore guide the Land-Rover 'Cambridge' across an improvised jungle bridge. It took the adventurers over six months to reach their destination.

▲ Barbara Toy's Land-Rover 'Pollyanna' still exists unchanged, cherished by enthusiast Tom Pickford. She covered hundreds of thousands of kilometres in the vehicle including two circumnavigations of the globe.

He was followed by Barbara Toy, an Australian writer, playwright, screenwriter and theatre director who came to Britain during the Blitz. She bought a Land-Rover which she christened 'Pollyanna' and followed in Townsend's tracks to Singapore, Australia and America. Remarkably, she repeated the adventure when in her eighties. She wrote a series of four books about her adventures in 'Pollyanna'.

▲ *Land Rover commissioned Dunsfold Land Rover to build a Land-Rover to commemorate the achievements of early explorers. It took part in the 13,000-kilometre 2012 'Journey of Discovery' from Solihull to Beijing.*

New Generations

Land-Rover sales grew steadily during the 1950s peaking at over 30,000 in the middle of the decade. However, it was the advent of a new model in 1958 that spurred demand to over 50,000 by the end of the 1960s. The new Series II looked very different from its predecessor, with wider-track axles demanding attention from the styling department. Rather than make the entire vehicle wider, Rover's Chief Designer David Bache chose to introduce barrelling of the body sides, creating the style that would last for nearly sixty years. However, this created a problem with sealing the doors that was never properly solved.

The Series IIA arrived in 1961 powered by a new range of petrol and diesel engines, later joined by a 6-cylinder petrol. The Series III was launched in 1971, a year in which Land-Rover production peaked at over 56,000. It introduced an all-synchromesh gearbox and a more modern facia that moved the instrument cluster in front of the driver.

LAND-ROVER SERIES III REGULAR PETROL	
Length	3620mm
Width	1680mm
Height	1970mm
Wheelbase	2240mm
Engine	Rover 2¼ Litre 4-cylinder petrol
Capacity	2286cc
Power	60kW @ 4250rpm
Torque	168Nm @ 2500rpm
Gearbox	Land-Rover LT76

◀ Rover developed a diesel engine for the Land-Rover in 1957 which was inherited by the Series II. It was not successful, however, and was soon replaced by a variant of the '2¼ Litre' engine family.

▶ This Short Wheelbase workhorse illustrates that the wider-track axles introduced with the Series II led to barrelled sides that became an iconic feature of Land-Rovers and Defenders thereafter.

▶ *The Series III retained the new position of the head and side lamps introduced on late model Series II vehicles to meet new lighting regulations. The new plastic grille was not universally popular.*

▲ *The Special Installations Department at Solihull assisted many specialist vehicle manufacturers to exploit the versatility of the Land-Rover. This HCB Angus fire appliance was a popular choice to deal with small-scale conflagrations.*

▶ *Echoing the original Land-Rover, the Series III 'Short' Soft Top was a great agricultural workhorse, although many farmers preferred the Pick Up which prevented uninvited livestock from joining them in the cab.*

▼ *The Series III 'Long' Station Wagon was extremely popular not least because its twelve-seater version was free of purchase tax in the home market. A car-derived 6-cylinder engine provided more power and a smoother ride.*

Expanding the Range

A reorganisation of the British Leyland conglomerate established Land Rover Limited as an autonomous business unit, allowing the company the freedom to begin determining its own future. The new management was quick to respond. A tranche of investment funding enabled the expansion of the all-alloy V8 engine production line leading to the launch of the Land Rover V8. Replacing the old side-exhaust-

LAND ROVER V8 STATION WAGON 1979	
Length	4580mm (with door-mounted spare wheel)
Width	1680mm
Height	2000mm
Wheelbase	2770mm
Engine	Land Rover All-Alloy V8
Capacity	3528cc
Power	68kW @ 3500rpm
Torque	225Nm @ 2000rpm
Gearbox	Land Rover LT95 Integrated Gear and Transfer Box

◄ *The High Capacity Pick Up used advanced material techniques to expand the load-carrying capability of the Land Rover.*

▶ *The County Station Wagon featured a brand-new, specially designed seat to cater for owners who wanted to use the Land Rover for more leisure-orientated pursuits.*

valve 6-cylinder and using a Range Rover permanent four-wheel-drive transmission, it was designed to take on the increasingly competitive challenge from the Toyota Land Cruiser.

Also aimed firmly at Japanese competition was the High Capacity Pick Up, which emulated the design of the Land Cruiser but used Land Rover's signature aluminium in the form of rolled sections and thin-wall castings. The County Station Wagon, with its new seating, chocolate paint work and side stripes, was aimed at the increasing leisure use of utility 4x4s and established a successful sub-brand.

▲ Installation of the V8 engine required a remodelling of the Land Rover engine bay and a new front end. Bright colours, taken from the Triumph sports car palette, increased its customer appeal.

▼ Powered by the V8 engine, the Land Rover could begin to rival the appeal of the popular Toyota Land Cruiser in overseas markets, but with the advantage of permanent four-wheel drive.

Coil Comfort – the One Ten and Ninety

The development of a new generation of Land Rovers was funded by a second tranche of investment money for the company and the programme was known as 'Stage 2'. To test the viability of using coil springs on a utility model, several 'hybrid' vehicles were constructed by placing Land-Rover bodies on Range Rover chassis, some of which were altered to give vehicles with 90-, 100- and 110-inch wheelbases. Testing at Eastnor Castle was impressive and the development programme was given the go-ahead.

It proved to be protracted and it was not until 1983 that the first of the new models, the One Ten, was launched. Its long-travel coil springs gave excellent off-road characteristics but body engineering and overall quality did not match this capability. The short-wheelbase Ninety, introduced a year later, incorporated many improvements including one-piece doors based on a design by Land Rover's Spanish subsidiary, Santana.

◀ *Some of the test hybrids, like this four-door 'command car', retained the Range Rover's 100-inch wheelbase. This was not adopted for production but prototypes were constructed in pursuit of overseas military contracts.*

▶ *Later One Ten models adopted the one-piece doors introduced with the Ninety. Station Wagons featured ride levelling like the Range Rover but build and engineering standards failed to impress Land Rover's new managing director, Tony Gilroy.*

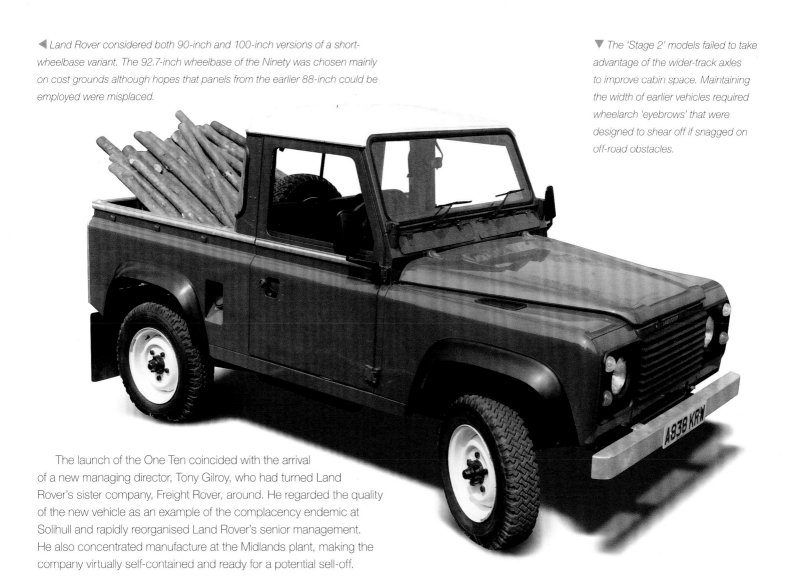

◄ *Land Rover considered both 90-inch and 100-inch versions of a short-wheelbase variant. The 92.7-inch wheelbase of the Ninety was chosen mainly on cost grounds although hopes that panels from the earlier 88-inch could be employed were misplaced.*

▼ *The 'Stage 2' models failed to take advantage of the wider-track axles to improve cabin space. Maintaining the width of earlier vehicles required wheelarch 'eyebrows' that were designed to shear off if snagged on off-road obstacles.*

The launch of the One Ten coincided with the arrival of a new managing director, Tony Gilroy, who had turned Land Rover's sister company, Freight Rover, around. He regarded the quality of the new vehicle as an example of the complacency endemic at Solihull and rapidly reorganised Land Rover's senior management. He also concentrated manufacture at the Midlands plant, making the company virtually self-contained and ready for a potential sell-off.

Stretching the Concept

The Land Rover 127 was almost literally 'designed on the back of a fag packet'. The author travelled to Australia for the bidder's conference for Project Perentie (see page 98) and saw the popularity of Japanese crew cabs. On returning to the UK, he used drawings being prepared for the upcoming One Ten to show how a Land Rover version could be built from existing components, although the resulting prototype used a shortened HCPU body so that a one-piece rear propeller shaft could be used.

Shown at the One Ten launch, the model found favour with the Southern Electricity Board who ordered sufficient numbers to warrant starting production. This initially took place in a special facility and later on line. The 127 was soon adopted by other utility companies and the suspension system was upgraded to allow greater loads to be carried. It also saw military service, being adopted as a support vehicle for the Rapier anti-aircraft missile system and is still used as the basis for the current field ambulance.

▼▶ *The Land Rover 127 became the Defender 130 in 1990. Its popularity meant it remained in production until the model's final week in January 2016.*

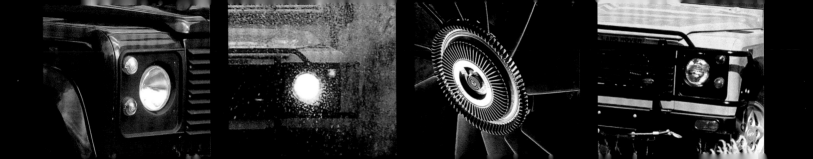

Defender Debuts

Research done as part of the Discovery programme revealed the value of the equity that lay in the Land Rover brand and considerable effort was invested in creating an image that would eventually support one of Britain's most successful companies.

Having a model with the same name as the overall marque was obviously not ideal and 'Defender' was chosen from a list of potential project codenames. The reaction of marketing focus groups proved positive and the name was decided upon, although the rights to it needed to be purchased from GKN Defence who had registered it for use on an armoured vehicle.

The introduction of the 200 Tdi engine into the Land Rover was selected as a suitable changeover point. There was considerable disquiet in the company's engineering department over the suitability of the power unit, first in Discovery and more vociferously in connection

LAND ROVER DEFENDER 110 Tdi STATION WAGON	
Length	4599mm
Width	1790mm
Height	2035mm (levelled)
Wheelbase	2794mm
Engine	Land Rover 300 Tdi 2.5-litre diesel turbocharged
Capacity	2495mm
Power	83kW @ 4000rpm
Torque	265Nm @ 1800rpm
Gearbox	Land Rover LT77

with utility usage cycles, such as towing and off-road capability. These concerns were swept aside and the Defender was launched with the new engine in late 1990. Offering 30 per cent more power and torque than the previous 2.5-litre diesel turbo combined with 30 per cent greater fuel economy, the new Defender was rapidly accepted by customers.

◄ The Defender was launched with a full model range known as the Defender 90, 110 and 130. While the name may have been new, it retained all the versatility of its predecessors.

◄ *The Tdi engine was developed under a programme codenamed 'Gemini' reflecting the fact that it was originally intended to have a petrol engine twin. The initial variant was the 200 Tdi – basically the earlier 2.5-litre diesel turbo with a direct injection cylinder head developed with the Austrian company AVL and an intercooler. The Defender installation initially differed from that of the Discovery and had less power, but it was replaced in 1994 by the 300 Tdi which was virtually a new engine. This gave the Defender more power and better refinement.*

Defender Defined

The Defender with its new, more efficient engine was well received with the name rapidly being absorbed into the Land Rover lexicon. But its introduction did not lift sales which were affected by a recession in the home market. It was also clear that, with its 1940s architecture, the Defender was seen as old-fashioned when compared with the Japanese competition. But, with the cancellation of the proposed replacement (see page 69), Land Rover was forced to upgrade the existing model as much as possible.

To extend its appeal, the County name was resurrected and applied not only to Station Wagons but also the 90 Hard Top in an effort to counter the inroads being made into the market by the popular Daihatsu Fourtrak. The interior was improved with new door trims and the repositioning of the front seats while standardising on power steering made a new, smaller steering wheel possible. An axle rationalisation programme enabled the fitment of alloy wheels from Discovery which further improved the Defender's look.

▶ With two decades of service to its credit, this Defender 90 still looks pristine although it has garnered an after-market decal and a body-coloured roof during its lifetime.

◀ While the option of Discovery-derived alloy wheels was quickly made available on the Defender 90, the 110 had to wait until a more robust design, capable of handling greater weight, evolved.

It was thought that the Discovery would replace the County Station Wagon, but demand for the latter persisted and the model was reintroduced in the early 1990s along with other County derivatives.

One of the biggest customer complaints concerned the lack of room in the Defender cab. In response, the outer front seats were relocated inboard, a smaller steering wheel was introduced and the door trims were redesigned.

◀ To counter Japanese competition, the County range was extended to the Defender 90 Hard Top. Featuring a station wagon roof, body-coloured 'eyebrows' and interior improvements, it was a popular model.

▲ While the balance had begun to shift towards the leisure market, utility models like the High Capacity Pick Up and 130 Crew Cab remained in the range, and in turn they received all the Defender improvements.

The improvements to the Defender worked, with production topping 36,000 in 1997, a level that would not be seen again. Positioned at the heart of the strong Land Rover brand, distinguished by its distinctive 'hockey stick' decal and powered by the definitive 300 Tdi engine, the model had never looked or sold better. A firm foundation had been laid for another two decades of Defender production.

Leisure Time

With the introduction of the Defender doing little to arrest the decline in sales and no replacement in the foreseeable future, Land Rover looked to expand the appeal of the model into new sectors.

The most distinctive of the leisure-orientated Defenders was a 110 for the American market. It was launched to mark the change of name of the US national sales company from Range Rover to Land Rover of North America. This was not primarily to sell Defenders but as a preliminary to the debut of the Discovery. Powered by a fuel-injected 3.9-litre V8, the model also featured a robust external roll cage, air conditioning and a premium in-car entertainment system.

Developed virtually in parallel were the Defender 90 North American Specification (NAS 90) and the SV90, which was created to show the home market that the Defender could be something other than a utility vehicle. Both had a soft top and a swing-away tailgate with spare wheel

◀ The Defender 90 was extremely popular in America thanks to its unique character. Initially launched as a basic vehicle that could be accessorised, the range grew to include Station Wagons with more powerful engines and automatic transmission.

▶ With its bright Caprice paintwork, the SV90 showed that Defenders could be fun. The hood was originally made by Tickford, but it fitted poorly and most were replaced. With only ninety built, extant examples are rare.

stowage. There the resemblance ended. The NAS 90 was powered
by a 3.9-litre V8, the SV90 by a 2.5-litre diesel, Land Rover engineers
having determined that the larger petrol engine was incompatible with
right-hand steering. And, while the American version
rode on chunky BF Goodrich tyres,
the SV90 had to make do
with standard rubber.

We'd love to tell you about the new Defender. Not now, of course.

On second thought, what better time to talk about how well the new 1995 Defender 90 Station Wagon handles tough driving conditions. With the brisk response of a 3.9-liter V8 engine, an internal and external safari cage, and permanent four-wheel drive, it's designed to take you in and out of the most threatening environments in a way that you can truly appreciate: A hurry. The new Defender also features a permanent hardtop with a pop-up sunroof and seating for six. What's more, it carries the formidable distinction of being a direct descendant of the original 1948 Land Rover. So why not call 1-800-FINE 4WD for the nearest Land Rover dealer? The Defender is priced at $32,000.* Do keep in mind that there are only 500 available. And even though it's a brand new vehicle, it already has a huge following.

DEFENDER 90

◀ Defender advertising in America was distinctively humorous, playing on the Land Rover's appearance in the TV series Daktari. The Station Wagon appeared for the 1997 model year just before airbag legislation forced the Defender out of the US market.

▼ Colour options for the NAS 90 Defender included AA Yellow, a name that Land Rover of North America insisted on keeping despite its possible negative associations. Accessories included detachable door tops and a 'bikini' canopy.

▼ *Only 534 Defender 110s were built for America, all but one in Alpine White. Originally selling for $39,900, the vehicle has now become a modern classic commanding prices several times that originally paid.*

Storm Force

While the Defender's iconic and well-loved profile remained reassuringly the same, 1998 saw a big change under the bonnet. This time the model would not have to wait for a new power unit. Instead it shared the limelight with its upmarket sibling, the Discovery, with a simultaneous launch of the high-tech Td5 5-cylinder engine.

Offering a significant power upgrade from the earlier Tdi, the Td5 also added refinement with its extra cylinder and high pressure Electronic Unit Injectors. And while many Defender enthusiasts were wary of its apparent complexity, the Td5 engine, codenamed 'Storm', was designed for worldwide service as it was able to tolerate poor fuels and run on a range of lubricants.

DEFENDER 110 1998 MODEL YEAR	
Length	3883mm
Width	1790mm
Height	2076mm
Wheelbase	2794mm
Engine	Land Rover Td5 5-cylinder diesel
Capacity	2493cc
Power	90kW @ 4200rpm
Torque	300Nm @ 1950rpm
Gearbox	Land Rover LT77 5-speed

Alongside the new engine came other power train upgrades including the option of the 'Q' for 'Quiet' derivative of the LT230 transfer box. This had new internals with revised gear tooth profiles alongside a new cable-operated gear change to reduce noise. Other new features included ABS brakes and Electronic Traction Control.

◄ *Originally designed for use by aid agencies, the Defender Double Cab joined the line-up in 2000. It became a popular derivative and the foundation for a number of limited editions.*

The Defender retained its iconic image while the Td5 engine gave it a useful performance upgrade, its presence being indicated by a discreet decal. Alloy wheels were a popular feature.

◀ *Codenamed 'Storm', the Td5 engine employed high-technology features and proved to be a rugged and reliable power unit. An acoustic cover embossed with Td5 and Land Rover logos enhanced the underbonnet appearance.*

▲ *The new power unit unfortunately did little to arrest the steady decline in Defender sales which were being eroded by the impact of the Discovery and pressure from competitors.*

The Td5 engine was the sole survivor of a family that was to include 4- and 6-cylinder variants. Designed in-house, Land Rover chose to use Electronic Unit Injectors, which precisely monitored the fuel entering each cylinder, rather than Common Rail system which the company felt was then not proven technology.

Much effort was put into making the new engine suitable for use in a variety of conditions. Surgical grade filters were employed in the fuel system while a centrifugal oil filter collected contaminants and extended the intervals between oil changes.

Twenty-First Century Defender

The familiar shape may have been the same but the 2002 model year Defender launched at the 2001 IAA Frankfurt motor show introduced some fundamental changes to its construction. Since its inception, Defender doors comprised an aluminium skin folded onto a steel frame. Use of metals of different chemical composition required strict application of barrier materials to prevent corrosion and the result was also often badly fitting. The 2002 model year Defender saw that change with the introduction of front, side and rear end doors formed from steel pressings. The new doors were of the same style but were easier to make, of more consistent quality and fitted better.

The new doors enabled the latest Defender to be specified with electric windows on the front set as well as a central locking system. Other touches of luxury included heated front seats and a heated windscreen. To accommodate the switches for these new features, the facia was upgraded with a new centre console that also housed a radio and CD player.

◄ *While the basics remained the same, the 2002 model year Defender facia had a new centre switch panel that housed the switches for new features such as the front electric windows, heated windscreen and headlamp levelling.*

▶ *The Defender's appearance may have been unchanged but the new steel doors made a big difference to the consistency and quality of the vehicle. The change also brought in improved seals to add a measure of refinement to the vehicle.*

◀▶ *Changes brought in for 2003 included a new model, the XS, which was distinguished from the others by alloy 'Boost' wheels and silver-finish front lamp surrounds.*

▼ *The new Station Wagon rear door featured a high-mounted stop lamp. Aluminium chequer plate for sills and wing tops was a popular accessory.*

Puma Power

With the introduction of the all-new Discovery 3, the Defender became the only user of the Td5 engine. With sales averaging fewer than 25,000 a year, this situation was clearly unsustainable and Land Rover's owners, Ford, looked for a substitute. They chose a variant of the 'Puma' Duratorq engine which was also used in the Transit van causing the revised Defender to be christened the 'Tranny Lanny'.

A 4-cylinder diesel engine of 2.4-litre capacity, the new power unit developed the same power as the outgoing Td5 but provided a useful 20 per cent increase in torque. This was handled by specifying a new Ford-Getrag 6-speed gearbox made at a factory at Halewood.

Ford demanded minimum change to the engine for the Defender installation so a revised bonnet with a 'power bulge' was required to allow the necessary clearance for front axle articulation.

DEFENDER 90 STATION WAGON 2007 MODEL YEAR	
Length	3894mm
Width	1790mm
Height	2021mm (with 235 tyres)
Wheelbase	2360mm
Engine	Ford 'Puma' Duratorq ZSD-242 2.4-litre diesel
Capacity	2401cc
Power	90kW @ 3500rpm
Torque	360Nm @ 2000rpm
Gearbox	Ford-Getrag MT82 6-speed

◄ The Ford 'Puma' Duratorq engine received Land Rover branding for its Defender installation. With its complex plumbing it was a tight fit and required a new bulged bonnet.

◄ The 2007 model year Defender also featured a striking new facia housing a new heater and air conditioning system with distinctive 'frog eye' air vents.

▶ A new engine for the Defender was a big event and one that required extensive testing. The regime included cold climate testing in the harsh environment of northern Sweden.

The Defender was renowned for its off-road ability and the boost in torque provided by the new engine was welcome. The new gearbox had a lower first gear for greater control in rough conditions.

▲ The Duratorq engine was canted upwards to give the front axle the required movement for off-road driving. A new pressed steel bonnet with a distinctive bulge was designed to replace the long-standing aluminium component.

The new engine was accompanied by significant changes to the Defender cabin which included a completely new facia with improved ergonomics and practicality although leg room remained a problem. Occupants now sat in stadium-style forward-facing seats.

Equally important was a new and much-needed heating and air conditioning system, the design of which proved extremely challenging given the space constraints imposed by the Defender's architecture which traced its origins back to the 1940s. Other changes, including revised propshafts, significantly improved the Defender's levels of refinement. The new gearbox had a higher top gear which finally gave the model a high-speed cruising ability.

▲ *The Defender 90 was modified to remove the bulkhead to allow access to the two forward-facing rear seats. The 110 model was available with five or seven seats. All featured three-point seat belts.*

◀ *A Utility variant of the Station Wagon was introduced in 2009. Replacing the rear windows with solid panels provided a functional concealed stowage area. Its re-classification as a commercial vehicle enabled businesses to reclaim VAT.*

Saving the Best Till Last

Even though the Defender DC100 concepts had debuted (see page 72) and an expected end date for the original model been declared, Land Rover announced a package of changes for the 2012 model year. The major feature of the upgrade was a new engine to meet EU5 emission standards. Another version of the Ford Duratorq, the new power unit was of 2.2-litre capacity but matched its predecessor for power and torque. To improve refinement it had a full acoustic cover while emission requirements were met by a particulate filter. The new engine had upgraded fluid seals, a fixed-vane turbocharger and single- rather than dual-mass flywheel. Other elements of the driveline remained unchanged.

Accompanying the new engine came a package of changes designed to improve overall levels of refinement. These included revised suspension bushes, upgraded door seals and a new acoustic pack. Attention to detail paid off with the Defender driving experience being considerably improved – even a degree of wind noise was audible for the first time. In its 2012 form, the Defender had reached its peak, but the end of the line was in sight.

◄ *Encompassing many detail changes, the upgrades for the 2012 model year Defender were a quantum leap in refinement. The model was now the best it had ever been, but was destined to remain in production for only a few more years.*

▶ *A final package of changes in 2013 introduced new premium seats, an upgraded entertainment system, a contrast roof option and new hood colour options for soft-top models.*

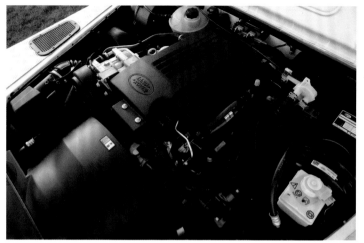

▼ The new engine was mated to the previous 6-speed gearbox and 2-speed transfer box. Incorporating a particulate filter in the exhaust system, components had to be re-arranged for the Defender installation.

▶ Land Rover Special Vehicles developed a customised Defender 110 Station Wagon to support vehicle launches and media events. Known as 'Bigfoot', it provided inspiration for the vehicles used in the James Bond *Spectre* movie.

▲ The new 2.2-litre engine was concealed by a new acoustic cover which, along with other changes, bestowed much improved refinement on the 2012 Defender.

Motoring media got their introduction to the 2012 Defender at an event where the highlight was a spectacular off-road night drive demonstrating that the Defender's all-terrain ability was as good as ever.

▼ The 2012 upgrades for the Defender transformed its driveability and refinement, but nothing could disguise the fact that the model was in the twilight of its production life.

The Making of Defender

The Defender was made in the same building at Land Rover's Solihull plant from 1948 until 2016. Components pressed from steel and aluminium were assembled in a facility once used to build Rover cars before being loaded onto special skids to progress through a state-of-the-art paint plant alongside other Jaguar Land Rover vehicles. Latterly the chassis, power train and other components were sourced from external suppliers with the bodywork and interior being assembled to them on a single production line. Production peaked at more than 56,000 vehicles in the 1970s with the Land-Rover Series III. Defender output achieved over 36,000 in 1997 but steadily declined thereafter.

▼ *The success of the Defender was down to its versatile modular construction. It also made it a demanding vehicle to build.*

▶ *While its appearance changed remarkably little over the years, the latest production techniques were employed to build the Defender.*

▲ *A vehicle set of body components is loaded on a skid for painting. Metallic finishes demand that the panels are aligned correctly.*

Chapter 4

Defender Concepts

DEF II

DEFENDER

FCrawley 31-10-90

Challenger Concept

Although it would eventually endure for another 25 years, at the start of the 1990s it was obvious that the Defender was approaching its sell-by date. The overseas markets had largely defected to Japanese products that were carving inroads into the home market with the Defender slipping from the top-selling slot in the utility sector.

Land Rover's reaction was the Challenger programme that would have become the Defender II. Based on a Discovery chassis and body platform, it used advanced materials in its construction. These included a composite roof for the hard-top and station wagon models and a front bumper designed to take hefty knocks. Challenger was not intended to meet the needs of the heavy duty market so the current Defender would have been built in a low volume facility for military and utility customers.

Nevertheless, Challenger was offered to the UK Ministry of Defence but this compromised the simplicity of the concept. This, and the general reluctance to proceed exhibited by the company's owners, British Aerospace, eventually led to the project being cancelled.

◄ *Designer Peter Crowley-Palmer's rendering of the Defender II used new panels on the Discovery body frame. However, the style did not appeal to diehard existing Defender owners.*

▶ *The sole survivor of the Challenger programme is a military prototype in the Dunsfold Land Rover Collection. Ironically, the complexity inherent in its development was a significant factor in bringing down the project.*

1999 SVX Concept

The Defender 'Special Vehicle X' concept was first shown at the IAA motor show at Frankfurt in 1999 as the conflict within BMW over the future of Rover Group reached its height. Although the publicity produced for the vehicle claimed that it was fitted with features such as ABS brakes, electronic traction control and Hill Descent Control as well as cross axle differential locks, many of these functions were inoperable. Finished in Himalayan Green, it stood out for its massive roll cage and huge 20-inch wheels with custom-made tyres.

The interior used a military instrument cluster and was heavily lined with aluminium chequer plate and festooned with equipment including a prominent fire extinguisher and a winch, while the oversize spare wheel took up much of the internal space. The driver and passenger sat in Recaro sports seats with full racing harness.

The SVX concept was later shown at Detroit and featured in a spectacular promotion video for the company. For many years the SVX was on display in the Gaydon styling studio where it served as a stimulus for Land Rover designers.

◀ *While a net kept equipment in place on the dash, the diff lock knobs were for decoration only as the equipment was not fitted.*

▲ *The SVX was posed on the Gaydon test circuit for its publicity photographs. To illustrate the issues BMW was having with the Rover Group, the shoot was a wholly German affair with a model being specially flown in for the occasion.*

▼ *Those big wheels hit the right note for the ultimate off-roader but a restricted turning circle made the SVX virtually unmanoeuvrable in the author's experience.*

DC100 Concept

Anticipation was high at the 2011 IAA Frankfurt motor show as the media gathered around the Jaguar Land Rover stand for their press conference. The Range Rover Evoque had debuted in Paris the year before and rumours abounded of another spectacular. The press corps was not to be disappointed, even if they had to wait as a change to the schedule put Land Rover at the top of the bill.

With lights flashing and smoke swirling across the stage the DC100 Concept made its appearance, introduced by Design Director, Gerry McGovern. A stubby short-wheelbase vehicle with a high waist and minimal overhang, the DC100 was said to be investigating 'the future design direction of the iconic Defender' with the designation coming from its 100-inch wheelbase.

But there was more. Land Rover staged a real coup when the DC100 Sport emerged alongside its sibling. Although said to take its conceptual cues from earlier canvas-roofed Land-Rovers, the DC100 Sport could not have looked more different with its sleek open style and crop of high-tech features.

▼ *Following its Frankfurt debut, driveable examples based on a Range Rover Sport chassis were developed to be driven by the press.*

▶ *The DC100's style owed little to earlier Land Rovers and Defenders, paving the way for a dramatic new look. Opinions, especially among diehard enthusiasts, were mixed.*

◄ The appearance of not one but two concepts was a big surprise as the DC100 and DC100 Sport were media stars. The Jaguar Land Rover stand was packed throughout the Frankfurt show. The company was obviously aiming at a wider market than strict utility use to justify a new Defender programme.

▲ Both concepts featured small design details that paid homage to earlier Land Rovers and Defenders. The air intake may have been ornamental but it echoed the earlier, purely functional design.

Both concepts trailed interesting new features that would soon reach production. This included a 2.0-litre petrol and diesel engine that would become Jaguar Land Rover's in-house 'Ingenium' power unit. Automatic Terrain Response would also soon debut on the new Range Rover and Range Rover Sport, as did a water depth 'wade sensing' function. Other features such as driver-activated spiked tyres and a wristband 'Leisure Key' have yet to appear.

The interior design echoed earlier models with a low centre console and three-abreast 'Social Seating' which could be folded to create more space and deployed to reveal concealed stowage. The multi-functional touchscreen was weatherproof and removable so that it could be used as a portable navigation device while recording high-defintion video. The trim fabrics used were from the latest range of sportswear and were said to be virtually indestructible, as well as being environmentally friendly. Leather hide also featured on the DC100 Sport as did Land Rover's signature aluminium. While revealing the DC100 concepts, Land Rover declared that a new Defender would be launched in 2015. Sadly, this target would be missed …

◀ *The interior had a low console area with multi-functional three-abreast seating. Both the latest fabrics and specially prepared hides were employed. The touchscreen was removable so that it could be used as an adventure tool with the zoom feature replacing binoculars.*

▶ *The DC100 Sport was clearly intended for a new leisure utility segment with markets in the Americas, Middle East and China very much in mind. This projected customer base was very different from the 'Warwickshire Farmer' that earlier models had been aimed at.*

Chapter 5

Sporting Defenders

Defender and the Camel Trophy

The first Camel Trophy was a one-off promotional event to publicise the well-known tobacco brand, but it then burgeoned into a full international off-road challenge. Land Rover was involved from 1981, fielding Range Rovers for the second event held in Sumatra. Land-Rover Series III vehicles were used in 1983 and the company then used the event to promote new models with the 110 featuring in 1984 and the 90 the year after that. With the advent of the Discovery, the Defender 110 was used in a support role. The event was won by the British team of Bob and Joe Ives in 1989 driving a Land Rover 110.

Taking place in remote parts of the world offering the most challenging of terrains such as the jungles of Borneo and Amazonia or the wastes of Siberia, the Camel Trophy was designed to test endurance as well as team work. It was not just a race, but also included elements of adventure expedition. The chance to compete was highly sought after and each participating nation conducted a rigorous selection process. Land Rover officially ended its association with the event after 1998 although Defender 110 HCPU (high-capacity pick up) supported Honda CR-Vs in the last event in 2000.

◀ Not strictly a Defender of course but the British team of Bob and Joe Ives won the Camel Trophy in this 110 Station Wagon in 1989. Event Land Rovers were finished in Sandglow paint and carried Camel decals.

▶ Training for the British Camel Trophy teams was undertaken at Land Rover's testing ground at Eastnor Castle which offered similar driving challenges to the event locations.

▲ Defender 110 Station Wagons acted as support vehicles for Freelanders during Land Rover's last Camel Trophy which took place in Tierra del Fuego in 1998.

▼ The Camel Trophy tested vehicles' capability to the utmost. Courage, perseverance and resilience – and not a little skill – were needed to get out of perilous situations like this.

G4 Challenge – Adventure Comes Home

When the Ford Motor Company acquired Land Rover in 2000, it was keen to exploit the wealth of experience that the brand had acquired. While the Camel Trophy had shared some undesirable associations with the tobacco industry, as well as some dubious environmental associations, it was certainly popular. Land Rover's own competition, the G4 Challenge, adopted some elements of the Camel event but incorporated an urban aspect to emphasise the breadth of capability of the vehicles.

The first G4 Challenge took place in 2003. No fewer than 31 Defenders were involved in the event that visited the USA, South Africa and Australia and included mountain biking, trail running and rock climbing as well as off-road driving in the full range of Land Rover vehicles. The eventual winner, Belgian fighter pilot Rudi Thoelen, declined the prize of a Range Rover, opting instead for a brace of Defenders. A second event took place in 2006 encompassing legs in Thailand, Laos, Brazil and Bolivia. A planned third G4 Challenge that would have taken place in Mongolia in 2009 was cancelled due to the prevailing world economic crisis.

◀ *Competitor selection and training took place at Eastnor Castle following in the tracks of the earlier Camel Trophy. The equipment carried in and on the vehicles was more diverse due to the more challenging and varied nature of the event.*

▶ *Defenders taking part in the G4 Challenge were finished in the event's signature Tangiers Orange paint and decal treatment. To commemorate the running of the first event, Land Rover offered the similarly equipped G4 Challenge Edition model.*

Land Rover changed the format of the G4 Challenge after the first event, with the second outing incorporating more vehicle-based activities. There were also concerns that the G4 Challenge was not as diverse as it should be and the planning for the 2009 event demanded that each participating nation should field male and female competitors. Land Rover also announced an association with the International Federation of Red Cross and Red Crescent Societies with the winning team's national branch receiving a vehicle in lieu of an individual prize.

◄ The Defender 110 Station Wagons built for the G4 Challenge were comprehensively equipped for the task with roof racks, a snorkel air intake and an array of auxiliary lights.

▲▶ A number of vehicles were prepared for the 2009 Mongolia event which was much anticipated by enthusiasts as it promised a return to more driving-orientated challenges.

Bowler Motorsport Defender Challenge

Bowler Motorsport under the direction of Drew Bowler had been adapting Defenders to complete in rally raid events such as the Dakar before a strategic partnership was announced with Land Rover in 2012. This led to the Defender Challenge which exclusively used Defender 90 Hard Tops in a seven-round series held around the UK.

The vehicles were prepared for the competition by Bowler Motorsport with modifications including a power and torque boost to the standard engine, upgraded suspension, a roll cage and a fire extinguisher system. The vehicles rode on Bowler Motorsport lightweight wheels with Cooper tyres. Defender Challenge vehicles were finished in a special livery and a special service package was also made available.

The Defender Challenge was conceived to offer a cost-effective route for drivers, navigators and service crews to gain the necessary experience and qualifications to take part in major international events such as the Dakar rally.

▲ The Defender Challenge 90 Hard Tops had a modified interior with racing seats, a roll cage and fire extinguisher system.

◀▶ Externally these sporting Defenders were distinguished by special bumpers and sill protectors complemented by a strikingly colourful paint scheme.

Bowler's Sporting Connection

The Bowler Motorsport story goes back to 1985 when company founder Drew Bowler began selling modified Land Rovers following his success in off-road competitions. His designs crystallised around the Bowler Tomcat which became an iconic rally raid mount. This led to the Wildcat which, although demonstrably a Defender, was based on a steel spaceframe clad in fibreglass panels. The model incorporated components from other vehicles in the Land Rover range such as the Discovery. A wide range of engines were offered including V8 petrol derivatives and re-mapped Td5 diesels. The Wildcat achieved considerable success in international events including the highest number of finishers in the 2005 Dakar rally.

The company moved on to create the Range Rover Sport-based models like the EXR while Land Rover cemented its relationship with Bowler who supplied vehicles for the Defender Challenge. Street-legal variants of the competition car, the Fast Road Defender, also feature in the Bowler catalogue.

◀ The Bowler Wildcat offered supreme off-road performance powered by boosted V8 petrol or Td5 diesel engines. Despite its distinctive Defender front end, the Wildcat featured spaceframe and fibreglass panel architecture.

▼ *The Bowler Fast Road Defender sports many features of the Defender Challenge model but in street-legal form. These include new lightweight wheels, an external roll cage, heated Recaro seats and an engine power upgrade.*

▲ Race2Recovery was set up in 2011 to give combat injured veterans the thrill of off-road competition. Using Bowler Wildcats, the team has achieved success in international rally raids.

▶ The Bowler Wildcat has become the vehicle of choice for many rally raid competitors, this example being crewed by brothers Javier and Miguel Grasa. It was one of several Wildcats competing in the 2015 Baja Spain.

Chapter 6

Defender in Service

Defender on the Front Line

The Defender and the Land Rover before it have a distinguished place in British military history. For many years the standard light and medium duty vehicles in the military fleet, the model evolved into specialist vehicles including the ½-tonne lightweight and 101 Inch 1-tonne Forward Control. An order for 8,000 of the latest generation of vehicles was placed in 1996. Developed under the code name 'Wolf', the contract encompassed Defender 90s and 110s, while Defender 130s to be completed as ambulances were ordered separately.

Wolf vehicles differed from their civilian counterparts to a considerable degree and were subject to vigorous testing to ensure that they could meet the demands of the military. Combat in Afghanistan and Iraq revealed certain shortcomings which resulted in upgrades to vehicle and occupant protection. Although the British Army quickly moved to larger armoured vehicles, the Defender remained still in demand thanks to it being more nimble in village streets and more discreet in tense situations.

◀ The Revised Weapons Mounted Installation Kit (RWMIK) variant of the Defender Wolf features enhanced protection, run-flat alloy wheels and upgraded Tdi engine. A wide variety of weapons including heavy machine guns can be carried.

▶ The Defender 'Snatch' armoured vehicle was originally developed to grab ring leaders of demonstrations in Northern Ireland. Sent to Afghanistan to combat insurgents, it was tactically unsuited to its new front-line role.

◀ Operating conditions in Afghanistan were extremely harsh. In addition there was a constant threat of attack and the need to be always on the alert for the presence of Improvised Explosive Devices (IEDs).

▶ British Army operations in Afghanistan also demanded that injured soldiers should receive treatment as soon as possible with the Defender Wolf 110 performing as a field ambulance.

▶ The US Army's 75th Ranger Regiment acquired variants of the Defender 110 to replace its Ford M151 'Mutt' vehicles. The Ranger Special Operations Vehicle (RSOV) family included this medical variant for rapid casualty evacuation.

Perentie – King of the Outback

Land Rover won a major contract to supply the Australian Armed Forces in 1987 with production running over into the Defender era. Known by the project name of 'Perentie' – a large Australian goanna lizard – two variants, a 110 and 6x6, were supplied in the face of competition from Jeep, Mercedes and Toyota. With a galvanised chassis, tough Isuzu diesel engine and an innovative third axle drive system for the 6x6, they were arguably the sturdiest Land Rovers ever. They served with distinction with the Australian Army and Royal Australian Air Force in Afghanistan and other theatres of operation.

LAND ROVER PERENTIE 6x6

Length	6140mm
Width	2220mm
Height	2760mm (over canopy)
Wheelbase	Axle 1-2: 3040mm, 1-3: 3940mm
Engine	Isuzu 4BD1T 3.9-litre diesel
Capacity	3856cc
Power	90kW @ 3600rpm
Torque	314Nm @ 2200rpm
Gearbox	Land Rover LT95 with third axle drive system

▲ Perentie vehicles were fitted with a 3.9-litre direct injection Isuzu diesel engine with 6x6 variants having a turbocharged version.

▶ The author's Perentie 110 Fitted For Radio (FFR) resides with his family near Perth, Western Australia. Perenties saw service with the RAAF as well as the Australian Army.

◀◀ The Perentie 6x6 featured a larger cab and a third axle drive system that used the power take-off mechanism of the LT95 transmission.

◀ Both variants of the Perentie saw service in various combat zones, notably in Afghanistan. The Australian SAS used a specially modified 6x6.

Workhorse of the World

Although in its later years Defender sales to the leisure sector predominated, it was at its heart a true utility workhorse. This was made clear during research on its possible replacement by a Discovery-based model (see page 68) when a French participant commented that 'It speaks its vocation'. The Defender's tough and versatile, no-compromise architecture made it the first choice for many organisations looking for a vehicle to fulfil specific roles in demanding conditions. These included utility companies in the UK and overseas that needed to transport crews to repair fallen power lines in remote locations, as well as motoring rescue organisations like the Automobile Association in the UK that had to reach unfortunate motorists who might be stranded in extreme weather conditions.

With the company traditionally supplying the vehicle of choice for adventurers seeking to explore remote parts of the globe, Land Rover's association with the Royal Geographical Society allowed the Defender to venture in the tracks of its forebears.

◀ Ubiquitous in rural hill farms, the compact size, short wheelbase and minimal overhangs of the Defender 90 Pick Up make it an ideal towing vehicle for the Ifor Williams double-deck sheep trailer.

▶ Defender 110s operated by the AA's Special Operations Response Team (SORT) were used extensively in the severe winter weather that recently affected the UK. Special equipment included battery packs and a kinetic energy recovery rope.

▶ *The Defender 130 is able to seat a work crew and carry their equipment. This well-furnished Environment Agency example is at work at Abingdon Lock, Oxfordshire.*

▼ *Defender Double Cabs are used in a Land Rover-sponsored programme to guard the coast of Denmark. Their all-terrain ability is especially valuable when it comes to negotiating the dune-lined sandy beaches.*

▼ Land Rover's support for the Royal Geographic Society included providing a Defender for an expedition to the 'Pole of Cold' in 2013. Located in Siberia, the location saw the lowest ever recorded temperature of -67.7°C in 1933. It is the coldest inhabited place known on Earth.

Defender for Aid and Conservation

Land Rover supports a number of organisations that use Defenders in the course of their work. Chief among these is the International Federation of Red Cross and Red Crescent Societies; this relationship stretches back to 1954. It culminated in 2008 when, to celebrate its sixtieth anniversary, the company presented the Societies with sixty vehicles for use around the world.

Another well-established partnership is with the Born Free Foundation which works to prevent captive animal suffering and protect threatened species in the wild. It became a Land Rover Global Conservation partner in 2002. A Land Rover vehicle operates as an elephant ambulance in Sri Lanka while Defenders assist in Born Free's anti-poaching operations in Kenya. They helped an operation to remove hundreds of snares and apprehend poachers within days of their arrival.

◄ *Born Free founder Virginia McKenna OBE has an unquenchable desire to protect wildlife, inspired by her role playing the famous naturalist Joy Adamson in the film* Born Free. *Projects include protecting the endangered Ethiopian Wolf.*

▲ *Biosphere Expeditions exists to promote wildlife projects where ordinary people work alongside scientists in the field. Many take place in remote areas where the Defender's rough-country abilities are exploited to the full.*

◀ Biosphere Expeditions many conservation projects include a study of leopards and caracals in South Africa. Others big cat programmes take place in Amazonia and it also studies the critically endangered snow leopard in Kirghizstan.

▲ Defender 130s were employed in the Russian Far East in programmes to protect the Siberian or Amur tiger that is critically endangered in the wild. The Defender played its part in extreme conditions to try and arrest the population decline of the animal.

Another of Land Rover's conservation partners is Biosphere Expeditions, a not-for-profit organisation for people seeking to offer their help to wildlife research and conservation projects. Given the importance of the Chinese market to Land Rover, the company also supports the China Exploration and Research Society which is active in exploring China's most remote regions. Another partner is Earthwatch, an international environmental charity.

▼ *Land Rover has a long-standing relationship with the International Federation of Red Cross and Red Crescent Societies. Defenders help not only overseas but also in the UK where the organisation responds to hundreds of emergencies every year.*

▶ *Land Rover's recent support of the IFRC has involved the loan or donation of nearly 120 vehicles. Globally, the company estimates that more than one million people have also benefitted directly or indirectly from Land Rover's support.*

Chapter 7

Defender at the Movies

Lara Croft: Tomb Raider

As Lara Croft the female hero of the *Tomb Raider* video game used a Land Rover, it was natural for her to be equipped with one of these vehicles for the 2001 movie starring Angelina Jolie as Lara. It was also a great opportunity for Land Rover's new owners, Ford, to leverage some publicity for their new acquisition.

The vehicle used in the filming, much of which was done at the UK's Pinewood Studios, was based on a Defender 110 High Capacity Pick Up finished in Bonatti Grey and fitted with a V8 petrol engine and automatic transmission. Three were built for the film with much of the work being done in Special Vehicles at Solihull.

Its appearance in the movie was fleeting although it was deemed significant enough to inspire a limited edition model. Its open configuration proved problematic when shooting on location as snakes and other wildlife fell into the Defender to the concern of the actress.

◀ *Lots of lights, a roll cage, a bonnet-mounted spare wheel and a winch gave the* Tomb Raider *movie Defenders a very purposeful look.*

▲ ▶ *Aluminium chequer plate abounded both inside and out while the dash arrangement came from a still secret military project.*

James Bond Defenders – *Skyfall*

The Defender made the screen again for the 2012 James Bond movie, *Skyfall*, appearing in a spectacular opening sequence filmed in Istanbul which rejected CGI in favour of live action. The vehicle was based on a seemingly standard Stornaway Grey Defender 110 Double Cab and seven vehicles were built for the sequence. In all, Jaguar Land Rover contributed no fewer than 77 vehicles to the production.

While the Defender was apparently driven by agent Eve played by Naomie Harris, it was in fact controlled by stunt driver Ben Collins, famous for his 'Stig' role in the BBC TV series *Top Gear*, sitting in a special roof-mounted cage. To offset the effect of the weight on the roof, extra stability was provided by extending the track and fitting special wheels. The engine had its power boosted and non-standard automatic transmission was installed. Defenders used in the production also had discreet internal roll cages to protect the occupants from genuinely dangerous situations during filming.

As well as its part in the film, a battered example of the Defenders used in the movie was featured in a window display at Harrods in London to publicise the opening night of the film. On its release *Skyfall* was a huge success breaking UK box office records.

◀ To publicise the opening night of the movie, a Defender used in the production of Skyfall appeared as part of special promotional display in a Harrods' window in London.

▶ While the Defender was apparently driven by Eve (Naomie Harris), it was actually controlled by stunt driver Ben Collins sitting in a roof-mounted pod.

▶ The movie Skyfall featured a spectacular multi-vehicle chase through the streets of Istanbul. While the hero emerged ready for action, 007's Defender was a little the worse for wear.

▼ *The Defender used in the opening action sequence of the movie was realistically 'distressed' for the part although, contrary to popular belief, the standard model is not bulletproof. Finished in Stornaway Grey and fitted with standard wheels, the Skyfall Defenders were chosen to look like a seemingly normal vehicle.*

TR 34 AR 1597

James Bond Defenders – *Spectre*

The Defender was back in 2015 for the 24th movie in the James Bond franchise, *Spectre*. Two Defenders appear in a snow chase sequence filmed in Sölden in the Austrian Alps where the evil Spectre henchman Mr Hinx has abducted Madeleine Swann (Léa Seydoux) in a Range Rover Sport SVR escorted by two Defenders. Bond pursues them in an Islander aircraft and none of the vehicles come out of the encounter well. Jaguar Land Rover also provided a C-X75 concept car used to chase Bond's Aston Martin DB10 around the streets of Rome. All the JLR vehicles used in the filming were displayed at the 2015 IAA motor show in Frankfurt supported by actor Dave Bautista who played Mr Hinx and Naomie Harris, cast as Miss Moneypenny.

The Santorini Black Defenders used for the film were based on the 110 Double Cab but the stand-out feature was their massive 37-inch Maxxis Trepador tyres mounted on special wheels and protected with wide wheelarch flares to give extra traction on the snow. A front protection bar flanked a bumper-mounted winch with a recovery rope being draped around the front of the Defender. A strong external roll cage with roof rack and auxiliary spot lamps together with a raised air intake completed the image of a strong, menacing vehicle.

◀ *Filmed here on a circuit in Surrey, England, the* Spectre *'Bigfoot' Defender 110s were more at home in the snow on location in Austria.*

▶ *In* Spectre, *the Defenders were driven by villains and they were presented in a threatening black finish to emphasise their sinister role.*

▼ The Spectre Defenders were based on the 'Bigfoot' specification that was developed for use by the Land Rover Experience team to provide off-road support to media and marketing events.

▼ The 37-inch wheels raised the ground clearance considerably, a factor which required a side step to make getting in and out easier.

Chapter 8

Defender Specials

Tomb Raider Special Edition

Land Rover was quick to follow up the appearance of the Defender in the *Tomb Raider* movie with a limited edition model. Just 250 were produced for sale in the UK using the 90 Station Wagon and the newly introduced 110 Double Cab as a basis for the design. Like the movie vehicle, the *Tomb Raider* Defenders were finished in Bonatti Grey but rode on unique Pewter Grey 'Boost' alloy wheels and were powered by the standard Td5 engine.

Special features included an external roll cage, a roof rack mounting quad driving lamps, a full-width rear step, side protection rails and a sump protection guard. Aluminium chequer plate was much used appearing on the bumper, wing tops, the sills and rear body. Chequer plate also featured on interior floor mats and seats were trimmed in specially-designed fabric. The steering wheel was covered in leather and a cast aluminium gear lever knob provided extra tactility.

◄ *Conceived for the 'urban adventurer', the Tomb Raider limited editions were distinguished by a neat cast 'Tomb Raider' roundel on the front wings and enhanced with aluminium chequer plate.*

▶ *The appearance of the Defender 90 Station Wagon was made even more distinctive by the addition of the Tomb Raider limited edition features, and it proved extremely popular with Land Rover fans.*

The extra equipment on the *Tomb Raider* limited editions was said to be worth £7,000 so it was little wonder that, combined with the publicity associated with the movie, it was much sought after. It cost £22,995 for the 90 Station Wagon – the 110 Double Cab carrying a £1,000 premium. This demand inspired many copies to appear on the market although original vehicles continue to command high prices.

▼ *The* Tomb Raider *limited edition copied many features of the Defender that was driven by Lara Croft in the eponymous movie, including a sump guard, chequer plate protection and grey paintwork.*

▶ *Adding to the tough image of the model, the 110 Double Cab variant of the* Tomb Raider *limited edition had an extension to the roll cage to protect the open rear load area.*

SVX Sixtieth Anniversary SE

The Sixtieth Anniversary of the Land Rover was celebrated with the launch of the Defender SVX special edition which debuted at the Geneva motor show in 2008. While taking many cues and its designation from the earlier SVX Concept (see page 70), the SVX Special Edition was designed to be actually driveable with standard size wheels, albeit of a unique design and fitted with chunky General Grabber TR tyres.

Just 1,800 were produced for sale worldwide in 90 soft-top and 110 station wagon versions. All bore a distinctive Santorini Black finish complemented by a matt decal treatment featuring a Sixtieth Anniversary graphic. The front seats were a bespoke Recaro design with the vehicle's occupants being serenaded by an upgraded in-car entertainment system with iPod™ connectivity. The driver was guided by a Garmin navigation system. Despite its macho appearance, power came from the standard 2.4-litre diesel engine.

▲ The SVX's distinctive grille badge celebrated sixty years of an iconic motoring marque.

◄◄ The SVX's massive external roll cage, tough side steps and Santorini Black finish echoed the design themes first explored in the SVX Concept of nearly ten years earlier.

▶ The front end design of the SVX was again obviously inspired by the earlier concept car with a unique grille and headlamp surrounds. The headlamps themselves were flanked by high intensity driving lamps.

The Defender SVX Special Edition also came in a 110 Station Wagon variant with many of the features of the soft-top model. The Defender Station Wagon always looked smart in black, the finish being complemented by its diamond-turned wheels, silver detailing and a distinctive contrasting decal on the SVX. The interior was specified to match with special Recaro seats and cast aluminium gear selector knobs. The vehicles were complemented by SVX merchandise including an aluminium key fob as a further attractive feature.

With a limited number being produced, owning one of the SVX Special Editions is proving to be a good investment.

▲ As well as the unique lighting arrangement on the front, the rear lights used LED technology for the first time on a Defender.

▶ The 110 Station Wagon proved a good canvas for the special Sixtieth Anniversary graphic developed for the SVX and which was carried on a contrasting matt finish decal.

Adventure, Luxury and Other Extremes

A series of limited editions marked a move away from its utility roots for the Defender. The 'Fire' and 'Ice' models of 2009 used the grille and headlamp surrounds of the SVX but rendered to match the striking colour ways of Vesuvius Orange or Alaska White set off by a Santorini Black roof and bonnet. The interior featured leather- and Alcantara-trimmed Recaro seats, again similar to those in the SVX.

The later Adventure Edition paid homage to the Defender's appearance in the Camel Trophy and G4 Challenge complete with snorkel air intake and expedition roof rack and ladder. Matching its off-road credentials, the Adventure Edition was shod with Goodyear MTR tyres mounted on special wheels with a contrasting black and diamond turned alloy finish. The interior was trimmed in leather including the seats and steering wheel. The model was offered in Yulong White and the striking Phoenix Orange both with a Santorini Black roof and bonnet.

▼ *The tough appearance of the Adventure Edition was underscored by a roof rack, snorkel, alloy sump guard, side sill protectors and Goodyear MTR tyres.*

▶ *The 'Fire' and 'Ice' models featured a similar front end treatment to the SVX albeit in a different finish. Production was limited to 850 that were sold in sixteen countries.*

The Adventure Edition was joined by the Autobiography and Heritage as the 'Celebration Series'. The Autobiography boasted a power upgrade that was shared with the 90 version of the Adventure Edition, but it gained a lavishly appointed interior trimmed in Windsor leather and deep pile carpet with aluminium door handles providing a smart finishing touch. Outside, the Autobiography featured a Santorini Black upper body and roof while the rest of the body could be finished in a choice of special colours.

The Celebration Series was completed by the Defender Heritage. Leaning heavily on cues provided by early Land-Rovers, the Heritage was finished in Grasmere Green with an Alaska White roof. The interior was trimmed in Almond cloth complemented by a body-coloured facia panel. The seats had a tag bearing the number of the first production Land-Rover, HUE 166, with the logo repeated on a bodyside decal. Only 500 Heritage Limited Editions were produced.

▲ *The Defender Autobiography was every inch the urban off-roader with its bespoke two-tone paint and luxury interior. Power was boosted by an upgrade to the standard engine tune.*

▶ *The Defender Heritage paid homage to Series Land-Rovers with its silver-painted front bumper replicating the galvanised finish of the original models.*

Defender LXV Celebration Special Edition

Land Rover formally moved into senior status when it celebrated its sixty-fifth birthday in 2013. To mark the event, the company gathered a range of its vehicles on the Packington Estate close to the factory at Solihull. The occasion was used to showcase the company's innovation over the decades although the Defender itself could be said to be largely 'unspoilt by progress'.

The Packington event also saw the debut of the Defender LXV Special Edition. Appropriately only sixty-five were available on the home market, all based on the 90 Hard Top derivative.

All the UK models were finished in Santorini Black with contrasting Corris Grey roof, grille and headlamp surrounds. The vehicle rode on grey-finished 16-inch Sawtooth wheels with the interior featuring full leather seats with an embossed LXV graphic. Leather with contrasting orange stitching also appeared on the centre console and steering wheel. The Defender LXV became highly sought after, commanding a considerable premium in the sales room.

▲ The signature graphic of the Defender LXV referenced the Land Rover's sixty-fifth birthday in Roman numerals.

◄ The Defender LXV looked very sleek with its black paintwork, metallic grey roof, subtle decal treatment and attractive wheels.

◀ *The company to which the original Land-Rover gave its name had come a long way in sixty-five years, and the Defender LXV Special Edition was a fitting tribute to seven decades of innovation.*

Rugby World Cup Trophy Transport

Land Rover sees the qualities needed to succeed in rugby as in line with its own core brand values and it has supported the game at all levels. Enrolled as the Official Vehicle Partner for the 2015 Rugby World Cup, the company made 450 vehicles available to provide transport for officials and guests at the various English venues. Most were the new Discovery Sport model but one Defender stood out. Developed by Land Rover Special Vehicles, it took the coveted Webb Ellis trophy on a 100-day 14,500km tour of the UK and Ireland before arriving at Twickenham rugby ground for the opening ceremony.

Based on a Defender 110 Station Wagon, the rear compartment was modified to create a cabinet for the trophy which required a controlled environment to protect its gilded silver finish. The Cup was illuminated by special lighting while added interest came via a 40-inch Toshiba screen showing scenes from the history of rugby.

◀ *The Webb Ellis Cup was protected by anti-glare security glass and kept visible by an anti-fogging climate control system.*

▼ *The interior featured black Windsor leather trim with gold contrast stitching, blue piping and an embossed Rugby World Cup logo.*

▼ *Rugby is a tough game and the trophy-carrying Defender reflected this through uncompromising black paint, a raised air intake, roof rack and bespoke wheels with off-road tyres, offset by a striking decal scheme.*

Fashion Icon – the Paul Smith Defender

Land Rover Design Director and Chief Creative Officer Gerry McGovern is well known for being immaculately dressed so, with this interest in fashion, a collaboration with Sir Paul Smith on a unique Defender was certain to result in something special.

Emerging in March 2015, the Paul Smith Defender did not disappoint. Its various panels featured twenty-seven individual colours matched from a swatch provided by Sir Paul for Jaguar Land Rover's Special Vehicle Operations. Taking inspiration from the British countryside as well as colours used by the Armed Forces, the Paul Smith Defender was resplendent in a kaleidoscope of muted blues, greys and greens neatly complemented by satin black wheels.

The interior was equally detailed featuring a mix of leather and Paul Smith cloth fabrics with contrasting stitching. Other touches included an image of keys inside the cubby box and a hand-painted bee on the roof to reflect the Defender's country heritage.

◀ *Taking inspiration from a number of sources, the Paul Smith Defender was packed with interesting details, the facia even incorporating a specially designed clock. The design process was recorded in a film screened during the 2016 London Fashion Week.*

▼ The exterior sported no fewer than twenty-seven different colours highlighting the patchwork nature of its construction. The colours were matched to a swatch supplied by the designer.

Electric Defender

Having declared that the Defender would shortly be replaced, Land Rover caught everyone by surprise when it revealed an all-electric variant at the 2013 Geneva motor show. In fact, the platform was in many ways ideal for the complex and heavy technology. The standard diesel engine and its accompanying gearbox were removed and replaced by a 70kW electric motor powered by a 300 volt, 27kWh lithium-ion battery which could be replenished in four hours using a fast charger. Energy was also generated by means of regenerative braking when using Hill Descent Control.

Drive was conveyed through a single-speed reduction gearbox connected to the standard transfer box and transmission. Control was enhanced by a specially programmed version of Land Rover's Terrain Response system. The battery alone weighed 410kg and was located in the engine bay. Despite some weight being saved by using air- rather than water-cooled components, the Electric Defender still turned the scales at 100kg more than the conventional variant. Later in the year, the Electric Defender entered service at the Eden Project visitor attraction in Cornwall pulling a road train around the site.

◀ The engine bay of the Electric Defender was taken up with a 27kWh lithium-ion battery which gave the technology demonstrator a range of 80 kilometres using its 70kW electric motor.

◀ Intended as a 'rolling laboratory' for electric power technologies, the Electric Defender was tested extensively on- and off-road. Uniquely for a Defender, its capability was boosted by a bespoke variant of the Terrain Response system.

▶ A pick-up version of the Electric Defender was used at the Eden Project in Cornwall to tow visitors in a four-carriage road train to the distinctive 'biomes'. Regenerative braking was used to charge the battery on the downhill trip.

Crafted by Kahn

Kahn Design was founded by Afzal Kahn in 1998 and quickly expanded from offering wheels and other accessories to producing complete vehicles at its Bradford headquarters. His Chelsea Truck Company was set up in 2013 to concentrate on Defender and Jeep variants. It boasts a boutique in Chelsea itself as well as a flagship showroom in Leeds. In recent years Kahn Design has gained an international reputation thanks to a presence at the prestigious Geneva motor show. It was here that Kahn's imposing 'Flying Huntsman' Defender 6x6 attracted considerable attention being favourably compared with the considerably more expensive Mercedes G-Wagen.

▲ *The Chelsea Wide Track Defender 90 Pick Up features 20-inch Defend Retro Dish wheels with 275/55 tyres finished to provide a striking contrast to its Keswick Green paintwork.*

▶ *Nearly a metre longer than the standard Defender 110, the Flying Huntsman 6x6 provides drive to all six wheels through a 6-speed automatic gearbox using push-button controls.*

▶▶ *The Station Wagon variant of the Chelsea Wide Track Defender 90 shows off its appliqué arches that accommodate 20-inch Mondial wheels finished in Nara Bronze.*

Totally Twisted

Twisted Land Rover was founded in 2001 by Charles Fawcett who was brought up with Land Rovers and ran his father's off-road driving centre. Twisted was originally set up as a subsidiary operation offering performance and tuning enhancements, but expanded rapidly as its reputation grew. By 2009, Twisted was focusing solely on the Defender and it remains confident that, despite the model's demise in 2016, it can continue working on existing stock, both new and used.

Based in North Yorkshire, Twisted offers a truly bespoke service using local craftsmen who produce a small number of Defender conversions each year to a very high standard. Driveline upgrades include reworking the standard engine to develop more power and torque. For even more performance Ford and General Motors engines are also offered. Interiors can be crafted in leather to suit customer's individual tastes.

◀ *This Defender 90 was crafted for a customer in the Far East. The modest exterior hides a GM 6.2-litre V8 petrol engine under the bonnet.*

▶ *The Twisted Ultimate Edition not only offered power upgrades for the production 2.2-litre engine but also a 3.2-litre Ford 5-cylinder engine from the same family.*

▲ The Twisted P10 upgrade for the Defender engine features an ECU re-map, upgraded air filter and bespoke intercooler and exhaust system.

▼ The Twisted Red Edition from 2012 had a striking interior trimmed in Hotspur Red leather including the high-backed seats, steering wheel, facia and centre console.

Startech – German Style

Notwithstanding its home-grown rival, the Mercedes G-Wagen, the Defender is perceived as the true icon of off-roading in Germany. Startech, a Brabus Group company, concentrates on enhancements to Land Rover and Range Rover products operating from its base in Bottrop in the German state of North Rhine-Westphalia. It also has branches in Irvine, California and Dubai.

Debuting at the 2013 Geneva motor show, the Defender Series 3.1 Concept paid homage to the model's heritage with a retro-style grille and 18-inch Monostar wheels designed to emulate the heavy duty steel originals. Other aspects were pure twenty-first century. Round 7-inch LED headlights flanked the grille while the Series 3.1 featured a media system developed with Sony Mobile that included two Sony tablet computers mounted in the front seat backs for rear compartment passengers, as well as providing internet access using Sony Xperia mobile phones. True to the Startech philosophy, the elements of the Series 3.1 are available for installation on existing vehicles.

◀ ◀ ▲ *The Series 3.1 interior was dominated by Recaro sports seats with built-in Sony tablet computers in their backs. The headlining was trimmed in black Alcantara fabric. The Series 3.1 featured external power mirrors while the Sony branding reflected the company's collaboration with Startech to develop the high tech infotainment and communications system.*

▼ The Startech Defender Series 3.1 styling was dominated by the retro-style grille, round LED headlamps and side lamps which, coupled with a white roof, emulated the iconography of earlier models. Tough side steps helped access to the cabin.

Chapter 9

Defender at the End of the Road

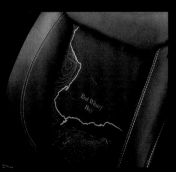

Defender 2,000,000

Land Rover Defender production reached the two million mark in 2015. To mark the occasion Land Rover built a unique bespoke design Defender 90 Station Wagon. While it was fabricated on the main production line at Solihull, the company recruited a special build team of celebrities to contribute to its assembly. Numbered among them was Jaguar Land Rover CEO Ralph Speth who fitted the unique VIN plate, adventurer and brand ambassador Bear Grylls who fitted the wheels and Commander Stephen Higham, the captain of the Royal Navy destroyer HMS *Defender,* who was appropriately made responsible for the 'monsoon' water test.

The Indus Silver Defender featured an engraving of a map of Red Wharf Bay where the original Land-Rover was conceived, special seats, black wheels and other unique details. The vehicle's registration plate commemorated its special identity and paid homage to the first production Land-Rover, HUE 166.

◀ *The unique high-backed seats bore a stylised map of Red Wharf Bay – a theme echoed on other parts of the interior – as well as the embroidered '2,000,000' distinction.*

▲ *The 2,000,000th Defender was marked by a unique cast aluminium plate. It was fitted to a panel marked by a line of spot welds and flanked by rivets – a characteristic of all Land Rovers and Defenders over nearly seven decades.*

The 2,000,000th Defender was finished in Indus Silver in homage to its aluminium construction, while a Red Wharf Bay graphic graced its front wings. Black wheels and other details provided an elegant contrast.

▼ *The 2,000,000th Defender was destined to be auctioned at Bonhams in London, the proceeds going to Land Rover supported charities including the Born Free Foundation. Before the sale, it was displayed in Dubai and photographed with a Series I Land-Rover against a backdrop of wind towers in the old city.*

▶ *On its return to London, the 2,000,000th Defender was exhibited alongside other Land Rovers before entering the sale room. The bidding rose to £400,000, a record for the model with the buyer coming from Qatar.*

The Last Defender

The last Defender rolled off the Solihull production lines on 29 January 2016 marking the end of sixty-eight years of production at the plant. The final vehicle was a Defender 90 soft top finished in Grasmere Green – as close as possible to the first models built in 1948. It was crowned by a special number plate, H166 HUE, a bow in the direction of the first official production Land-Rover, HUE 166.

The event was attended by more than 700 past and present Land Rover employees who had been involved with the Land Rover and Defender over its long run. Each was presented with a specially engraved aluminium hood cleat said to be the same component as that used from the inception of the model.

The last Defender was earmarked to be retained by the company in its new collection of historic vehicles. Land Rover also announced its new Heritage Restoration Programme in which a team of experts will restore and breathe new life into Series Land-Rovers.

◄ ▲ *The normally calm and efficient Defender production line became a media scrum as the last of a long line neared the end of the track.*

▼ The very last Defender off the
Solihull production lines after a
sixty-eight-year run stands in the now
redundant South Works facility. The
total number of Defenders and its
forebears produced are recorded as
2,016,933 vehicles.

The last Defender was assembled in the same building that housed the original production line. South Works at Solihull had been built more than seventy-five years previously as 'Shadow Factory No. 1' to assemble aircraft engines. Once heavily camouflaged, South Works still bears remnants of the original paint. With massive worldwide demand for the Jaguar, Land Rover and Range Rover vehicles built in the plant, space is at a premium.

With the demise of the Defender the Land Rover range lost its keystone model. Fleet and utility users will now have to turn to other manufacturers to fulfil their needs while those offering luxury conversions are scouring the world for unsold stock or turning to previously owned vehicles. However, rumours of overseas manufacture continue to circulate. As the last Defender rolled off the line, Land Rover remained tight-lipped about the next generation of its utility line but did disclose that 'it would be recognisably a Defender'.

▲ The last Defender was adorned with a grille badge replicating the 'pilchard tin' style of earlier models. The dates show that it was originally planned for production to cease in 2015. Demand led to a short reprieve but the badge wasn't corrected.

◄ With hazard lights flashing, the last Defender is driven off the line.

▶ HUE 166, the first production Land-Rover, led a parade around the Solihull site to celebrate sixty-eight years of the Defender.

Index

Acknowledgements

The publisher and author would like to thank the following for their assistance in the preparation of this book: Jaguar Land Rover's Land Rover press office, Australian Department of Defence, British Motor Museum, Kahn Design, Bowler Motorsport, Twisted Land Rover, Brabus/Startech, The AA, US Department of Defense, Glenn Smith, James Taylor.

Page 8: HUE 166, the first Land-Rover, chassis number LR01.

Page 34: The SV90, first of the leisure Defenders.

Page 46: The 90 Station Wagon the iconic amalgam of leisure and utility.

Page 66: The DC100 Sport – high tech Defender for the digital age.

Page 78: Making a splash on the Defender Challenge.

Page 92: Army stalwart – the Defender 'Snatch' protected vehicle.

Page 108: Gangster getaway – 'Bigfoot' Defender from Spectre.

Page 120: SVX – spirit of Defender.

Page 148: £400,000 Defender – the 2,000,000th auctioned for Born Free.

While every effort has been made to credit contributors and copyright holders, the publisher would like to apologise should there have been any omissions or errors and would be pleased to make the appropriate correction to future editions of the book.

Picture credits

All pictures © Jaguar Land Rover, with the exception of the following:

British Motor Museum courtesy of Jaguar Land Rover: pages 11 below, 12, 14, 15, 22, 24 below right, 27 above right, 27 below right, 31, 36, 37.

Mike Gould: pages 10, 11 above, 17, 18, 19 left, 20 right, 27 left, 34, 39, 43, 69, 70 left, 71, 99, 102 above, 154 left, 157 above.

Dunsfold Collection courtesy of Mike Gould: page 19 right.

Land Rover courtesy of James Taylor: pages 38, 40.

Land Rover courtesy of Mike Gould: pages 41, 42, 50, 68, 70 right, 81 above right, 81 below right.

Land Rover North America courtesy of Mike Gould: pages 42, 44.

Australian Government Department of Defence © Commonwealth of Australia: pages 98 left LAC David Said; 98 right Capt Alan Green.

Wikimedia Commons (Creative Commons Licence): pages 45 Vetatur Fumare; 113, 114 Thesupermat.

Wikimedia Commons (Defense Imagery, Public Domain): pages 94 Efren Lopez, US Air Force; 96 below Mr. Michael Lemke, Department of Defense Civilian, US Military.

Wikimedia Commons (Defence Imagery MOD, Open Government Licence): pages 92 Cpl Russ Nolan RLC; 95 LA(Phot) Dave Griffiths; 96 above Harland Quarrington/MOD; 97 Sergeant Alison Baskerville RLC.

Flickr.com (Creative Commons Licence): pages 104 right Land Rover Our Planet © Biosphere Expeditions; 105 left Land Rover Our Planet © Biosphere Expeditions.

Shutterstock.com: page 91 Rodrigo Garrido.

The Automobile Association (The AA): page 101.

© Bowler Motorsport: pages 86 left, 88, 89.

© Kahn Design: pages 142, 143.

© Twisted Automotive: pages 144, 145.

© Startech/Brabus® Group: pages 146, 147.